from SEA TO SHINING SEA

PENNSYLVANIA

By Dennis Brindell Fradin

CONSULTANTS

Ken Finkel, Curator of Prints, The Library Company of Pennsylvania

Robert L. Hillerich, Ph.D., Professor Emeritus, Bowling Green State University;
Consultant, Pinellas County Schools, Florida

 CHILDRENS PRESS®
CHICAGO

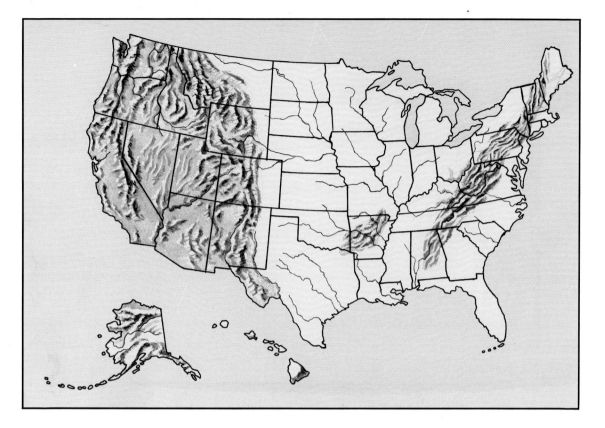

Pennsylvania is one of the three Middle Atlantic states. The other Middle Atlantic states are New York and New Jersey.

For my friends, Bob and Jaynie Wilcox

Front cover picture: The Golden Triangle, Pittsburgh; page 1, Pennsylvania Dutch country; back cover, Ganoga Falls, Rickett's Glen State Park

Project Editor: Joan Downing
Design Director: Karen Kohn
Typesetting: Graphic Connections, Inc.
Engraving: Liberty Photoengraving

THIRD PRINTING, 1994.

Library of Congress Cataloging-in-Publication Data

Fradin, Dennis B.
  Pennsylvania / by Dennis Brindell Fradin.
    p.   cm. — (From sea to shining sea)
  Includes index.
  ISBN 0-516-03838-9
  1. Pennsylvania—Juvenile literature. [1. Pennsylvania.]
I. Title. II. Series: Fradin, Dennis B. From sea to
shining sea.
F149.3.F68   1994   93-32757
974.8—dc20   CIP
                                                          AC

Table of Contents

A unit dressed as colonial militia celebrates Constitution Day in Philadelphia

Introducing the Keystone State

P ennsylvania is in the northeastern United States. It is one of the smaller states. But it has the fifth largest number of people. Pennsylvania is nicknamed the "Keystone State." It was in the middle of the first thirteen states.

A keystone is the stone in the middle of an arch. It holds the other stones in place.

Pennsylvania has a rich history. The Declaration of Independence was written there. So was the United States Constitution. It set up the country's government. One of the Civil War's bloodiest battles was fought in Pennsylvania.

Today, Pennsylvania is a leader in many fields. It produces large amounts of coal, steel, chocolate, and apples. Two major United States cities, Philadelphia and Pittsburgh, are in Pennsylvania.

The state is special in other ways. Where did Benjamin Franklin live? Where were flag-maker Betsy Ross, President James Buchanan, and television's Fred Rogers born? Where is the world's largest mint for making coins? Where is the Little League World Series played? The answer to these questions is: the Keystone State.

Overleaf: Hawk Mountain Bird Sanctuary

A picture map of Pennsylvania

DUNNINGTON

Mountains, Rivers, and Woods

MOUNTAINS, RIVERS, AND WOODS

*P*ennsylvania is one of three Middle Atlantic states. New York and New Jersey are the other two. Lake Erie and New York form Pennsylvania's northern border. New Jersey and part of New York are to the east. Delaware, Maryland, and West Virginia are to the south. Ohio and part of West Virginia are to the west.

Pennsylvania covers 45,302 square miles. That makes it bigger than only seventeen of the forty-nine other states. Most of Pennsylvania's land has mountains, hills, and valleys. The Allegheny, Blue

Left: Loyalsock River Canyon, in the Appalachian Mountains Right: Allegheny National Forest, in western Pennsylvania

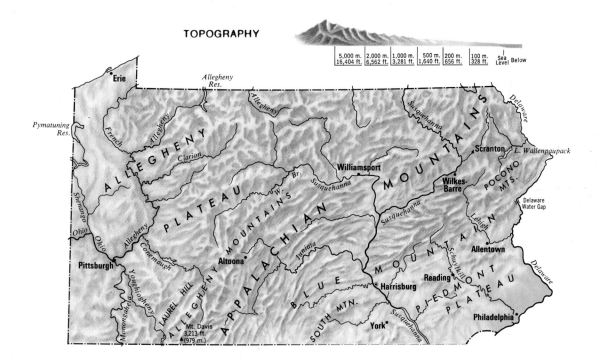

| 5,000 m. 16,404 ft. | 2,000 m. 6,562 ft. | 1,000 m. 3,281 ft. | 500 m. 1,640 ft. | 200 m. 656 ft. | 100 m. 328 ft. | Sea Level | Below |

Ridge, and Pocono Mountains cover much of the state. The Alleghenies have Pennsylvania's highest point. That is Mount Davis. It is 3,213 feet above sea level. Rich, flat farmland is in the southeast and in the northwest along Lake Erie.

RIVERS AND LAKES

Pennsylvania looks like a rectangle with a ragged eastern edge. There, the zigzagging Delaware River forms the border. Another major river is the Ohio. It starts in Pittsburgh. The Ohio is formed where the Allegheny and Monongahela come together. Pennsylvania's other rivers include the Susquehanna, Juniata, and Conemaugh.

Pittsburgh's Three Rivers Stadium stands near where the Ohio River begins.

9

Lake Erie splashes against northwestern Pennsylvania. One of the five Great Lakes, it covers about 10,000 square miles. Several hundred small lakes lie within the state.

WOODS AND WILDLIFE

About three-fifths of Pennsylvania is covered with forests. The hemlock is the state tree. Oaks, walnuts, pines, and sycamores also grow there. Pennsylvania has the largest Norway maple and the largest Norway spruce in the United States. Wildflowers brighten Pennsylvania's woods and meadows. The mountain laurel is the state flower.

Left: The Youghiogheny River Right: A Rickett's Glen State Park waterfall, in the Appalachian Mountains

The white-tailed deer is the state animal. Foxes, raccoons, black bears, and skunks also live in Pennsylvania. The ruffed grouse is the state bird. Wild turkeys and ring-necked pheasants are found there, too.

Ferns and forest in the Appalachians

The ruffed grouse is noted for the drumming noise it makes with its wings.

CLIMATE

Pennsylvania has hot, rainy summers. Temperatures over 90 degrees Fahrenheit are common. Parts of Pennsylvania get about 40 inches of rain each year.

Pennsylvania's winters are cold and snowy. Temperatures then can dip below 0 degrees Fahrenheit. Parts of the state receive 7 feet of snow each winter.

Overleaf: Militiamen at Washington Crossing State Park reenact Washington's Crossing of the Delaware.

From Ancient Times Until Today

FROM ANCIENT TIMES UNTIL TODAY

About 300 million years ago, Pennsylvania was swampland. Over millions of years, plants in the swamps were turned into coal and oil. Few states have as much coal as Pennsylvania.

The Ice Age began about 2 million years ago. Glaciers then covered Pennsylvania's northern third. The glaciers' melting ice left behind small lakes.

AMERICAN INDIANS

The first people reached Pennsylvania more than 10,000 years ago. The Ice Age was just ending. These early people were hunters. They traveled about following herds of animals.

Many years later, the Delaware Indians became a major Pennsylvania tribe. They lived along the Delaware and Brandywine rivers. The Delawares grew corn, beans, and squash. They also hunted deer. The Delawares were peaceful. They served as judges when other tribes fought.

Three other tribes also lived in Pennsylvania by the 1600s. The Susquehannocks lived along the

The Delaware Indians (above) called themselves the "Lenape." That means "original people." Europeans called them the Delawares.

Susquehanna River. The Eries lived along Lake Erie. The Monongahelas lived along the Monongahela River.

EUROPEAN EXPLORERS AND COLONISTS

Henry Hudson arrived in Delaware Bay in 1609. Although he was English, Hudson worked for a Dutch trading company. By the 1620s, the Dutch controlled the fur trade with the Indians.

The people of the Netherlands are known as the Dutch.

Sweden was the first country to settle and farm Pennsylvania. The Swedes began New Sweden along the Delaware River in 1638. At first, they, too, were only interested in trading for furs. In 1642, Johan Printz came to govern New Sweden. In 1643, Printz founded Fort New Gothenburg. This was Pennsylvania's first non-Indian town. It stood on Tinicum Island near present-day Philadelphia. Swedish farmers and crafters made homes there. However, New Sweden never had more than several hundred settlers.

The Dutch captured New Sweden in 1655. They made it part of New Netherland. New Netherland also included Delaware, New Jersey, and New York. Again, there was little growth. By 1660, fewer than 1,000 settlers lived in Pennsylvania.

WILLIAM PENN'S COLONY

By the 1660s, England had colonies north and south of New Netherland. In 1664, England seized New Netherland. Pennsylvania passed to English rule. But few settlers arrived until 1681. In that year, King Charles II of England gave Pennsylvania to William Penn. That is when Pennsylvania got its name. *Pennsylvania* means "Penn's woods."

Penn was a Quaker. This faith preached peace and kindness. Most of England's colonies had only people of certain faiths and countries. Penn welcomed everyone to Pennsylvania. Quakers moved there. So did Catholics, Jews, Lutherans, and others. They came from England, Wales, Germany, Scotland, Switzerland, and other countries.

By the late 1700s, one-third of all Pennsylvanians were of German heritage. That was the highest percentage of Germans in the thirteen colonies.

In 1682, Penn founded Philadelphia. *Philadelphia* is a Greek word meaning "city of brotherly love." Penn also made treaties of friendship with the Indians. In 1689, the world's first Quaker school was founded in Philadelphia. Today, it is called the William Penn Charter School.

As more settlers came, they moved west of Philadelphia. Lancaster was laid out in 1730. York was laid out in 1741. But Philadelphia remained Pennsylvania's main city.

Benjamin Franklin helped make Philadelphia a great city. He founded America's first successful lending library in Philadelphia in 1731. It still exists. Franklin also helped start the country's first general hospital there in 1751. The Pennsylvania Hospital is still open today also.

In the 1750s, England and France fought for control of North America. This was called the French and Indian War (1754-1763). Many Indians helped France. The American colonists helped England. George Washington led Americans in the war's first battle. It was fought in 1754 near present-day Uniontown. The next year, the English army was soundly defeated. The battle took place near present-day Pittsburgh. Nearly 1,000 soldiers on the English side were killed or wounded.

In 1758, English troops built Fort Pitt. It was the start of the city of Pittsburgh. From there, the English gained control of the west. Finally, five years later, England won the war.

THE REVOLUTIONARY WAR

The French and Indian War cost England much money. England then put new taxes on the colonists. The colonists felt that this was unfair.

This Fort Pitt and Blockhouse marker in Point State Park marks the start of the city of Pittsburgh.

They wanted to break free from England. To do this, the Americans fought the Revolutionary War (1775-1783).

For most of the war, Philadelphia was the American capital. There, the Continental Congress named George Washington to lead the American army. In Philadelphia, on July 4, 1776, Congress issued the Declaration of Independence. It said that the colonies had become the United States of America. The building where the Declaration was issued is called Independence Hall. Bells rang out the good news.

Independence Hall

Two big Revolutionary War battles took place in Pennsylvania. George Washington and his army lost both of them. The Battle of Brandywine was

Below: The Battle of Brandywine

General George Washington and his French aide, the Marquis de Lafayette (with red scarf), at Valley Forge

fought near Philadelphia on September 11, 1777. The Battle of Germantown was fought on October 4, 1777. Germantown is now part of Philadelphia. By October 1777, the English controlled Philadelphia. Congress left town and moved the capital to York (1777-1778).

After Germantown, Washington led his army to Valley Forge. This is west of Philadelphia. They spent the winter there. About 3,000 men died of cold, hunger, and disease. Baron Friedrich von Steuben, a Prussian military man, came to help Washington. He turned the Valley Forge survivors into a good fighting force. In 1783, the United States finally won the war.

THE NEW GOVERNMENT AND A NEW STATE

American leaders met in Philadelphia in 1787. They wrote the United States Constitution. It states the framework of the country's government. Pennsylvanians provided ideas for the Constitution. Some of those Pennsylvanians were Benjamin Franklin, James Wilson, and Gouverneur Morris.

Delaware approved the Constitution on December 7, 1787. By so doing, it became the first state. Pennsylvania became the second state on December 12, 1787.

Philadelphia was Pennsylvania's first state capital. The city was also the United States capital during the 1790s. George Washington lived in Philadelphia as the first president. The United States Congress met at Philadelphia's Congress Hall. That is next to Independence Hall.

George Washington was president from 1789 to 1797.

In the late 1700s, settlers reached central and western Pennsylvania. The state capital was moved to be closer to more people. Lancaster replaced Philadelphia as the state capital in 1799. Then, in 1812, Harrisburg became the permanent capital. In

1800, Washington, D.C., replaced Philadelphia as the United States capital.

The young state became a leader in transportation. John Fitch of Bucks County built the country's first working steamboat. He tested it along the Delaware River in 1787. The Philadelphia-Lancaster Turnpike was finished in 1794. It was the country's first hard-surface highway. In 1829, the first locomotive in the United States ran on Pennsylvania railroad tracks. The *Stourbridge Lion* made the historic run.

Fitch's steamboat went only 3 miles per hour.

Improved transportation helped Pennsylvania grow. By 1850, the state had 2,311,786 people. New York was the only state with more people.

Mining was also important to the Keystone State. By the mid-1800s, Pennsylvania provided most of the country's coal. In 1859, Edwin Drake drilled an oil well near Titusville. Oil spouted from the well that August. This marked the start of the oil industry.

THE FIGHT TO END SLAVERY

A replica of the world's first oil well, near Titusville

Pennsylvanians were among the first Americans to fight slavery. In 1775, the Quakers began the country's first antislavery society. In 1780, Pennsylvania

A Civil War battle is reenacted at Neshaminy Park, in Philadelphia.

passed a law to end slavery in the state. Other northern states ended slavery, too. By 1850, northerners wanted the South to end slavery, too.

In 1857, Pennsylvanian James Buchanan became president of the United States. He wasn't interested in fighting slavery. The next president was Abraham Lincoln, from Illinois. He didn't want slavery to spread to the new western states. Southerners feared he would outlaw slavery in their states. The southern states left the Union. This led to the Civil War (1861-1865). It was fought between the North (the Union) and the South (the Confederacy).

About 340,000 Pennsylvanians served the North. In July 1863, North America's biggest bat-

Only New York sent more troops than Pennsylvania to fight for the North.

21

tle was fought at Gettysburg. About 25,000 soldiers on each side were killed or wounded. On November 19, 1863, President Lincoln made a great speech at the battlefield. It is called the Gettysburg Address. Lincoln ended the speech with this wish: ". . . that government of the people, by the people, and for the people, shall not perish from the earth."

The North won the Civil War in 1865. The slaves were freed that year. About 35,000 Pennsylvanians died helping to win the war.

STEEL, COAL, AND LABOR UNIONS

After the Civil War, Europeans poured into Pennsylvania. They came from Italy, Poland, and Russia. These people found work in Pennsylvania's steel mills, coal mines, and factories. By 1900, the state's population had grown to 6,302,115.

During those years, Pennsylvania helped the United States become an industrial giant. Andrew Carnegie opened the country's first big steel plant near Pittsburgh in 1873. Pittsburgh became a great steelmaking center. People called it the "Steel City."

Pennsylvania steelworkers and coal miners worked long hours. Their pay was low. The coal mines were dangerous. Between 1870 and the early

Andrew Carnegie

1900s, almost 10,000 Pennsylvania miners lost their lives.

The Molly Maguires fought for the coal miners' rights. They killed a number of mine officials. In 1877, ten Molly Maguires were put to death for murder. Labor unions worked more peacefully for workers' rights. In 1902, the coal miners went on strike. At the strike's end, they received an eight-hour day. They also got a 10 percent pay raise.

Coal miners coming out of a mine at the end of a long workday

WORLD WARS AND DEPRESSION

In 1917, the United States entered World War I (1914-1918). More than 370,000 Pennsylvanians were in the armed services. The state's steel mills turned out warships and weapons.

During the war, the radio industry grew. Armies kept in touch through radio messages. After the war, the first scheduled broadcast in the world came from Pittsburgh. On November 2, 1920, Pittsburgh station KDKA broadcast the presidential election results.

U. S. troops on their way to Europe during World War II

In 1929, hard times hit the country. This was called the Great Depression (1929-1939). Pennsylvania coal miners and steelworkers were badly hurt. In some towns, four of every five workers lost their jobs. Some Pennsylvanians starved to death.

In 1941, the United States entered World War II (1939-1945). This helped end the depression. Pennsylvania's industries sprang to life. The state's steel and coal helped win the war. So did the more than 1 million Pennsylvanians who were in the armed services.

About 27,000 Pennsylvanians lost their lives in World War II.

Recent Successes and Problems

Since World War II, Pennsylvania has enjoyed many successes. In 1956, the Pennsylvania Turnpike was completed. This was the country's first superhighway. More visitors poured into the state. New hotels and motels were built.

In 1957, the country's first major nuclear power plant opened in Shippingport. That is near Pittsburgh. These plants make electric power. In 1979, Pennsylvania was the site of a nuclear accident. That March, the Three Mile Island plant near Harrisburg leaked radiation. People had to leave the

The Three Mile Island nuclear power plant

area. No one died. However, the accident led to safer ways for running these plants.

Some Pennsylvania black people and women have held high government posts. Edith Sampson of Pittsburgh served in the United Nations (UN) from 1950 to 1953. Sampson was the United States' first black delegate in the UN. Philadelphian Robert Nix was elected to the United States Congress in 1958. He was Pennsylvania's first black member of Congress. In 1959, Anne Alpern became Pennsylvania's attorney general. She was the first woman attorney general in the fifty states. In 1983, W. Wilson Goode was elected Philadelphia's first black mayor. Sophie Masloff became Pittsburgh's first woman mayor in 1988.

During these years, Pennsylvania has also had problems. Pollution is one of them. Pennsylvania factories have sent harmful chemicals into the air and water. Lead and other chemicals have hurt the Delaware River. Pennsylvania also has about 100 hazardous waste dumps. They could cause health problems if they aren't handled right.

In the 1970s, the steel industry ran into trouble. Other countries made cheaper steel. Pennsylvania's steel mills were out of date. Many shut down. Steelworkers lost their jobs. Other

Edith Sampson

industries also suffered. By 1993, nearly one Pennsylvania worker in ten was jobless.

The shortage of jobs has been a blow to the state's big cities. Pittsburgh lost 50,000 people between 1980 and 1990. Philadelphia lost twice as many people. Like other big cities, Pennsylvania's cities face problems of poverty, crime, and drugs.

Yet, Pennsylvania continues to move ahead. Philadelphia and Pittsburgh have built new convention centers. The rebuilt Pittsburgh International Airport opened in 1992. These and other projects will bring more business and more people to Pennsylvania.

In 1987, Pennsylvania celebrated 200 years of statehood. Few states have as proud a history. Today, Pennsylvanians also look forward to a bright future.

In Philadelphia, balloons formed a flag and bands played patriotic songs at the bicentennial celebration of the U.S. Constitution.

Overleaf: A girl showing her Guernsey cow at the Bedford County Fair

Pennsylvanians and Their Work

PENNSYLVANIANS AND THEIR WORK

As of 1990, nearly 12 million people lived in Pennsylvania. Only California, New York, Texas, and Florida had more people. About 88 of every 100 Pennsylvanians are white. About 10 in every 100 are black. Only 2 in every 100 are Hispanic. A small but growing number of American Indians and Asians also live in Pennsylvania.

Most Pennsylvanians live in big cities. Yet, nearly 4 million live on farms or in small towns. No other state has that many rural people. The Keystone State is a rather safe place to live. By the early 1990s, only four states had a lower crime rate.

About 10 percent of Pennsylvanians are black and more than 1 percent are Asian.

THEIR WORK

More than 5 million Pennsylvanians have jobs. Over 1 million of them make products. Foods are the top product. Hershey Foods makes chocolate candy. Packaged fruits and vegetables, cookies, and ice cream also come from Pennsylvania.

Pennsylvania is one of the top five makers of steel, carpets, and clothing. It is among the top ten

makers of many other goods. They include medicine, paint, glass, motor oil, and machinery.

More than 1 million Pennsylvanians sell goods. More than 1.5 million provide services. They include hotel workers, nurses, doctors, and lawyers. Philadelphia is well known for its law firms. The old term "Philadelphia lawyer" is used to describe a good lawyer anywhere.

About 100,000 Pennsylvanians are farmers. The state ranks fifth at producing milk. That is its top farm product. Pennsylvania leads the country at growing mushrooms. It is among the top ten grow-

Pennsylvania is a leader at growing peaches (left) and mushrooms (right).

Many Pennsylvanians work at mining coal.

ers of apples, grapes, and peaches. Oats, snap beans, sweet corn, tomatoes, and cherries are other important crops. Pennsylvania chickens lay 5 billion eggs a year. That is 20 eggs for each American. Only California and Indiana produce more eggs. Turkeys, horses, and hogs are also raised in Pennsylvania.

Almost 30,000 Pennsylvanians work at mining. Most are coal miners. Pennsylvania ranks fourth at mining coal. The Keystone State is a leader at producing crushed stone. Oil, natural gas, and iron are other Pennsylvania mining products.

Overleaf: A dairy farm near Somerset

A Trip Through
the Keystone State

DRINK MILK!

A Trip Through the Keystone State

*P*ennsylvania is a wonderful place to visit. Many visitors enjoy its small towns, its big cities, and its historic sites. Others come to ski or hike in its highlands. Still others sail or canoe along Pennsylvania's waterways.

Philadelphia

This statue of William Penn is on top of city hall in Philadelphia.

Philadelphia is in the state's southeast corner on the Delaware River. It is Pennsylvania's biggest city. Only four United States cities are larger.

Atop city hall stands a statue of William Penn. It is 37 feet tall. It is the biggest statue on top of a United States building. To honor Penn and other early settlers, Philadelphia is called the "Quaker City." It is also called the "City of Brotherly Love." But many people just call it "Philly."

Some of Philly is new. The 945-foot tower at One Liberty Place was finished in 1987. It is the state's tallest building. Yet, its historic sites are what make Philadelphia special.

Independence Hall was the country's birthplace. Visitors can see where the Declaration of

Independence and the Constitution were signed. The Liberty Bell is housed nearby.

The Philadelphia skyline

From there, it is a short walk to the Betsy Ross House. Betsy Ross made some early American flags. Some think she made the very first American flag there in 1777.

Philadelphia has many great museums. The Academy of Natural Sciences was founded in 1812. It is the country's oldest science museum. The Pennsylvania Academy of Fine Arts is the oldest United States art museum. It dates from 1805.

Philadelphia also has the world's largest mint. Visitors to the Philadelphia Mint can see coins being made.

The Liberty Bell

Philadelphia has four pro sports teams. The Eagles play football and the 76ers play basketball. The Flyers are the hockey team, and the Phillies play baseball.

William Penn lived north of Philadelphia. His farm is called Pennsbury Manor. Visitors can tour the reconstructed home and gardens today.

Valley Forge National Historical Park is west of Philadelphia. George Washington's 1777-78 winter headquarters still stands. His men's huts have been rebuilt.

Washington's Headquarters, Valley Forge National Historical Park

Southeastern Pennsylvania

Southeastern Pennsylvania has most of the state's people. In this part of the state lie five of Pennsylvania's largest cities. They are Bethlehem, Reading, Allentown, Lancaster, and Harrisburg.

One of America's oldest log structures is in Bethlehem. It dates from 1758. Today, Bethlehem is known as an old steelmaking city.

Nearby is Allentown. It is known for making trucks. In 1777, the Liberty Bell was hidden in an Allentown church. The English had captured Philadelphia that year. The Americans didn't want the Liberty Bell to fall into enemy hands. Today, visitors view the Liberty Bell Shrine. It is in the Zion United Church of Christ.

West of Allentown is the Hawk Mountain Bird Sanctuary. Eagles, falcons, hawks, and vultures can be spotted there.

To the south is Reading. Thomas Penn helped found the town in 1748. He was William Penn's son. Daniel Boone was born outside Reading in 1734. Boone lived there until he was sixteen. Today, visitors can tour the Daniel Boone Homestead.

To the south is Lancaster. Many German people settled there. They were called Pennsylvania Dutch.

Daniel Boone's birthplace

The Germans brought *fraktur* writing to Pennsylvania. *Fraktur* is fancy, heavy black and red lettering. Designs of stars, birds, and flowers decorate the letters. The Pennsylvania Dutch used *fraktur* for writing wedding and birth records. A few southeastern Pennsylvania artists still do *fraktur*.

Many Lancaster County people belong to the Amish faith. The Amish live simply. They do not use telephones or electricity. They can still be seen traveling by horse and buggy.

The Landis Valley Museum is in Lancaster. The old buildings there bring pioneer days to life. Wheatland is also in Lancaster. It was President James Buchanan's home (1848-1868).

A few miles southwest is York. It was the United States capital in 1777-78. Today, visitors enjoy touring the Harley-Davidson motorcycle plant. They also can visit the Wrestling Hall of Fame.

Gettysburg National Military Park is southwest of York. Visitors can explore the battlefield. The Eisenhower Farm is near the battlefield. Dwight Eisenhower was the thirty-fourth president of the United States. He spent his last years at the farm.

North of York is Harrisburg. It was founded in 1785. Today, Harrisburg is the state capital.

The Pennsylvania Dutch are really Pennsylvania Germans. Deutsch is the German word for "German." Deutsch was mispronounced and became "Dutch."

Amish farms in Lancaster County

38

Pennsylvania's lawmakers meet at the state capitol. The State Museum is also in Harrisburg. It has displays on Pennsylvania history and wildlife.

A few miles east is Hershey. What may be the world's only Chocolate Avenue is there. Hershey's street lamps are shaped like Hershey Kisses. Chocolate World has tours that show how chocolate products are made.

SOUTHWEST PENNSYLVANIA

Groundhog Day (February 2) has ties with Punxsutawney, Pennsylvania. Punxsutawney Phil, a

A Hershey Kiss street lamp in the town of Hershey

The state capitol

Fort Necessity National Battlefield and stockade near Uniontown

well-known groundhog, lives there. If a groundhog sees his shadow that day, spring is supposed to be far off. If it is cloudy and he can't see his shadow, spring is near. Television and radio broadcasters visit Punxsutawney each February 2. They report whether or not Punxsutawney Phil saw his shadow.

To the south is Johnstown. A dam near Johnstown collapsed on May 31, 1889. A wall of water rushed toward the town. More than 2,200 people died. The Johnstown Flood Museum has objects rescued from the flood. The museum even has a bottle of the floodwater.

To the southwest is Uniontown. Nearby, George Washington built Fort Necessity in 1754. Today, the rebuilt fort looks like it did then.

To the north is Pittsburgh. It is the state's second-biggest city. Fort Pitt, dating from 1758, was the start of Pittsburgh. Part of the fort still stands in Pittsburgh's Point State Park.

Pittsburgh was once known mainly for steel. Now, it is also a medical center. In 1953, Dr. Jonas Salk worked at the University of Pittsburgh. He made a vaccine against polio. Today, Pittsburgh's hospitals are leaders in organ transplants.

Pittsburgh's downtown is called the Golden Triangle. It is shaped like a triangle. Beautiful skyscrapers rise above it. The 841-foot USX Tower is the city's tallest building.

Pittsburgh has a great orchestra. Pittsburgh's people are proud of the Carnegie Museum of Natural History. Its dinosaur collection is one of the world's best. Young people love Pittsburgh's Children's Museum. There, they can visit a copy of the set from "Mister Rogers' Neighborhood." That program comes from Pittsburgh.

NORTHWEST PENNSYLVANIA

Northwest Pennsylvania was the birthplace of the United States oil industry. The Drake Oil Well Museum is near Titusville. A full-size model of Edwin Drake's oil well is there.

To the north is Erie. This city is on Lake Erie. It was settled in 1795. Erie has almost 110,000 people. That makes it the state's third-biggest city.

Erie played an important part in the War of 1812 (1812-1815). Warships for Oliver Hazard Perry were built there. In 1813, he used them to defeat the British. This was at the Battle of Lake Erie. Perry reported the victory from his ship, the *Niagara*. "We have met the enemy, and they are ours," he said. Today, the *Niagara* is docked in Erie.

The USX Tower

41

Allegheny National Forest covers about 800 square miles of northwest Pennsylvania. It is nearly the size of the state of Rhode Island.

NORTHEAST PENNSYLVANIA

Near Wellsboro is Pine Creek Gorge. This natural wonder is a 50-mile-long, 1,100-foot-deep canyon. Waterfalls add to its beauty.

South of Pine Creek Gorge is Williamsport. Families with Little Leaguers enjoy visiting that city. It is the home of Little League Baseball. Each August, the Little League World Series is played there. The Little League Museum has displays on the league's history. It honors well-known people

A Little League baseball game

who were once Little Leaguers. Two of them are Nolan Ryan and Tom Seaver.

A double waterfall in Delaware Water Gap National Recreation Area

To the northeast is Scranton. It is the state's fifth-biggest city. Scranton used to be a big coal-mining center. Today, the Lackawanna Coal Mine offers underground tours of a once-working mine. Steamtown is a Scranton train museum. Trains dating back to 1887 can be seen there.

The Pocono Mountains are east of Scranton. This is a favorite resort area. At the eastern edge of the Poconos is the Delaware Water Gap. This is a good place to end a Pennsylvania tour. The Delaware River dug this beautiful valley millions of years ago. People go there today to canoe, hike, and camp.

Overleaf: Benjamin Franklin

A Gallery of Famous Pennsylvanians

A Gallery of Famous Pennsylvanians

Many Pennsylvanians have become famous. They include authors, artists, athletes, and explorers.

Benjamin Franklin (1706-1790) was born in Boston. He moved to Philadelphia in 1723. There, he became a printer, scientist, inventor, author, and statesman. Franklin did a well-known experiment with a kite. He proved that lightning is electricity. He also wrote many sayings, including "Early to bed and early to rise, makes a man healthy, wealthy, and wise." Franklin also helped write the U.S. Constitution and the Declaration of Independence.

Anthony Wayne (1745-1796) was born in Chester County. He was a Revolutionary War general. People called him "Mad Anthony" because he fought fearlessly. Waynesburg, Pennsylvania, is one of many cities named for him.

Stephen Foster (1826-1864) was born in Pittsburgh. He wrote many beautiful songs. They include "O Susanna" and "My Old Kentucky Home."

Henry John Heinz (1844-1919) was also born in Pittsburgh. When he was young, Heinz made

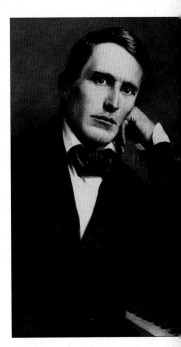

Songwriter Stephen Foster

catsup and horseradish. He used vegetables from the family garden. Later, his H. J. Heinz Company became a giant food maker. In 1896, he coined the slogan "57 Varieties" for the company.

Robert Peary (1856-1920) was born in Cresson. He was an explorer with the U.S. navy. Peary made many trips to the Arctic. In 1909, he led the first group that reached the North Pole. Peary wrote four books about his trips.

Elizabeth Cochrane Seaman (1867-1922) was born near Pittsburgh. She became a newspaper

Explorer Robert Peary

reporter. Seaman wrote under the name "Nellie Bly." She took that name from a Stephen Foster song title. In 1889-90, Bly traveled around the world alone in record time. She wrote a book about her trip. It is called *Nellie Bly's Book: Around the World in Seventy-two Days.*

Pennsylvania has produced many fine artists. **Benjamin West** (1738-1820) was born in Springfield. One of his best-known paintings is *Penn's Treaty with the Indians.* It can be seen at the Philadelphia Museum of Art. West taught art to **Charles Willson Peale** (1741-1827). Although born in Maryland, Peale later lived in Philadelphia. He painted more than 1,000 pictures of well-known people. They included pictures of George Washington and Benjamin Franklin.

Artist Charles Willson Peale

Mary Cassatt (1844-1926) was born in what is now Pittsburgh. Many of her paintings show love between mothers and children. **Henry Ossawa Tanner** (1859-1937) was also from Pittsburgh. He moved to Philadelphia when he was twenty-five. Tanner drew animals at the Philadelphia Zoo. He became the first black American artist to become well known.

Philadelphia-born **Alexander Calder** (1898-1976) came from a family of sculptors. He invented

Concert singer
Marian Anderson

the "mobile." That is a sculpture that moves in the air. **Andrew Wyeth** was born in 1917 into a family of artists. They lived in Chadds Ford. When he was only twelve, Wyeth illustrated the book *Robin Hood*. Later, he became known for his paintings of the countryside.

Daniel Hale Williams (1858-1931) was born in Hollidaysburg. He became a doctor. In 1893 in Chicago, Williams operated on a man. He had been stabbed in the heart. Williams saved the man's life. This was the first open-heart operation. Williams was black. He made it possible for many black nurses and doctors to be trained.

Marian Anderson (1902-1993) was born in Philadelphia. As a young girl, she earned money singing at church concerts. Anderson became one of the world's greatest concert singers. But because she was black, Anderson was kept from singing in Constitution Hall. That was in 1939 in Washington, D.C. Instead, she sang outdoors at the Lincoln Memorial. More than 75,000 people heard her sing.

Bayard Rustin (1910-1987) was born in West Chester. He was a black American who was raised as a Quaker. Rustin helped organize the 1963 March on Washington. The 200,000 marchers sought equal rights for black Americans.

Louisa May Alcott (1832-1888) was born in Germantown. It is now part of Philadelphia. As a

Author Louisa May Alcott

Astronaut Guion Bluford, Jr.

child, Alcott kept what she called an "imagination book." She later wrote *Little Women* (1868). It is about four sisters during the Civil War. Alcott served as a nurse during that war.

Rachel Carson (1907-1964) was born in Springdale. She became a scientist and author. Carson studied wildlife at Hawk Mountain. She wrote *Silent Spring* (1962). It explains how certain chemicals can harm the environment.

Guion Bluford, Jr., was born in Philadelphia in 1943. In 1983, he became the first black American in space. Bluford was an astronaut aboard the space shuttle *Challenger*.

Many baseball stars have come from the Keystone State. **Honus Wagner** (1874-1955) was born in Carnegie. He became a great shortstop for the Pittsburgh Pirates. Wagner won a record eight National League batting titles. Pitcher **Christy Mathewson** (1880-1925) was born in Factoryville. He won 373 games. Only two pitchers ever won more. Slugger **Hack Wilson** (1900-1948) was born in Ellwood City. He holds the season record for runs batted in. He knocked in 190 in 1930. **Stan Musial** was born in 1920 in Donora. He won seven batting crowns. "Stan the Man" had an amazing .331 lifetime average. **Reggie Jackson** was born in Wyncote in 1946. He earned four home-run titles. The Reggie candy bar was named for him.

Pennsylvania athletes come in all sizes. **Willie Hartack** was born in Johnstown in 1932. He was only 5 feet 3 inches tall. Hartack became a jockey. He rode five Kentucky Derby winners. **Wilt Chamberlain** was born in Philadelphia in 1936. At over 7 feet tall, he became a basketball star. "Wilt the Stilt" averaged 50 points per game in 1962. Once that year, he scored 100 points in a game. Both are NBA records.

Pro football's all-time scorer is from Youngwood. **George Blanda** (born 1927) scored a record 2,002 points. Tennis great **Bill Tilden** (1893-1953) was born in Germantown. He led the

Basketball star Wilt Chamberlain (right)

Football player George Blanda

51

United States to seven Davis Cup wins. **Arnold Palmer** was born in Latrobe in 1929. He became a great golfer. Palmer made golf exciting to watch. His fans were called "Arnie's army."

Movie star **James Stewart** was born in Indiana, Pennsylvania, in 1908. He won an Academy Award for best actor. It was for *The Philadelphia Story.* His best-known film is *It's a Wonderful Life.* **Grace Kelly** (1929-1982) came from Philadelphia. She won the Academy Award for best actress. It was for her role in *The Country Girl.* In 1956, she married a prince. Kelly was then called Princess Grace of Monaco.

Actress Grace Kelly later became Princess Grace of Monaco.

Two great dancers were born in Pittsburgh. **Martha Graham** (1894-1991) danced on stage. She helped create modern dance. **Gene Kelly** (born 1912) danced in the movies.

Philadelphian **Bill Cosby** was born in 1937. He co-starred in the television show "I Spy" (1965-1968). That made him the first black person to star in a network show. From 1984 to 1992, millions watched him on "The Cosby Show."

Fred Rogers was born in Latrobe in 1928. He is the creator and host of "Mister Rogers' Neighborhood." "There's only one person in the whole world like you," Mr. Rogers tells his young viewers. "And I like you just the way you are."

The birthplace of Fred Rogers, Marian Anderson, Reggie Jackson, and Mary Cassatt . . .

Home also to William Penn, Benjamin Franklin, Charles Willson Peale, and Andrew Carnegie . . .

The place where the Declaration of Independence and the United States Constitution were written . . .

Today, a leader at coal mining, steelmaking, and apple and grape growing . . .

This is Pennsylvania—the Keystone State!

Dancer Martha Graham

Did You Know?

Pennsylvania has towns called North East and Library. North East is in northwest Pennsylvania. Library has no library.

Root beer was first made in the United States in Philadelphia in 1866. Philly was also the birthplace of the ice-cream soda in 1874.

In 1874, the Philadelphia Zoo became the nation's first zoo that was open to the public.

Pennsylvania also has towns named California and Indiana. Other towns with unusual names include Snow Shoe, Slippery Rock, Paint, Bird-in-Hand, Big Beaver, Mars, and Moon Run.

Hershey Foods makes about 33 million Hershey Kisses each day. It takes about 50,000 cows to produce the milk used for one day's worth of Hershey's milk chocolate.

The popular children's magazine *Highlights for Children* is based in Honesdale.

The 1889 Johnstown Flood was the reason for the first major relief effort of the American Red Cross. Clara Barton, the organization's founder, ran Red Cross efforts in Johnstown.

Israel Jacobs of Pennsylvania was the first Jewish member of the United States House of Representatives. He began serving in 1791.

Until 1947, black players were not allowed in major-league baseball. Some all-black teams were as good as major-league clubs. The Pittsburgh Crawfords were one of the best baseball teams ever. Crawfords stars included Satchel Paige, Cool Papa Bell, and Josh Gibson.

The world's longest stone-arch railroad bridge is near Harrisburg. Rockville Bridge is almost 3,800 feet, or three-fourths of a mile, long.

The first pro football game was played in Latrobe near Pittsburgh in 1895. Latrobe won 12-0 against a team from nearby Jeannette. Nearly 100 years later, the Pittsburgh Steelers became the first football team to win four Super Bowls (1975, 1976, 1979, and 1980).

Roadside America is an unusual attraction in Shartlesville. Its tiny houses, trains, and other models show how America has changed over 200 years. Laurence Gieringer began building the models in 1903 when he was about ten years old. He continued building them for more than fifty years.

Each year, the Philadelphia Mint issues more than 6 billion coins worth about $300 million a year. Most of them are pennies.

57

PENNSYLVANIA INFORMATION

State flag

Mountain laurel

Ruffed grouse

Area: 45,302 square miles (thirty-third among the states in size)

Greatest Distance North to South: 175 miles

Greatest Distance East to West: 306 miles

Borders: Lake Erie and New York to the north; New York and New Jersey to the east across the Delaware River; Delaware, Maryland, and West Virginia to the south; West Virginia and Ohio to the west

Highest Point: Mount Davis, 3,213 feet above sea level

Lowest Point: Sea level, along the Delaware River in southeast Pennsylvania

Hottest Recorded Temperature: 111° F. (at Phoenixville, northwest of Philadelphia, on July 10, 1936)

Coldest Recorded Temperature: -42° F. (at Smethport, in northwestern Pennsylvania, on January 5, 1904)

Statehood: The second state, on December 12, 1787

Origin of Name: Pennsylvania means "Penn's woods"; the name honors the family of William Penn; *sylvania* is from a Latin word meaning "woods"

Capital: Harrisburg (since 1812)

Previous Capitals: Chester (1681-1683), Philadelphia (1683-1799), and Lancaster (1799-1812)

Counties: 67

United States Senators: 2

United States Representatives: 21 (as of 1992)

State Senators: 50

State Representatives: 203

State Motto: "Virtue, Liberty, and Independence"

Nicknames: "Keystone State," "Quaker State"

State Seal: Adopted in 1791

State Flag: Adopted in 1907

State Flower: Mountain laurel

State Bird: Ruffed grouse

State Tree: Hemlock

State Animal: White-tailed deer

State Dog: Great Dane

State Insect: Firefly

State Fish: Brook trout

Hemlock trees

Mountains: Allegheny, Blue Ridge, and Pocono ranges (all in the Appalachian Mountains)

Some Rivers: Delaware, Ohio, Allegheny, Monongahela, Susquehanna, Juniata, Conemaugh

Some Lakes: Lake Conneaut, Raystown Lake, Lake Erie

Wildlife: White-tailed deer, foxes, raccoons, black bears, skunks, opossums, weasels, minks, muskrats, ruffed grouse, cardinals, blue jays, robins, wild turkeys, Canada geese, eagles, many other kinds of birds, brown trout, bass, many other kinds of fish

Manufactured Products: Chocolate products, beer, bread, cookies, many other foods, paint, medicine, many other chemicals, computers and other machinery, carpets, steel, glass, clothing, watches and clocks, paper, books, farm machinery, motor vehicles, refined oil, toys and sporting goods, jewelry and silverware, musical instruments

Farm Products: Milk, mushrooms, apples, grapes, peaches, snap beans, sweet corn, tomatoes, cherries, pears, plums, strawberries, tobacco, oats, hay, cut flowers, eggs, chickens, turkeys, horses, hogs, beef cattle,

Mining Products: Coal, crushed stone, limestone, sand and gravel, oil, natural gas, iron

Population: 11,881,643, fifth among the states (1990 U.S. Census Bureau figures)

White-tailed deer

Major Cities (1990 Census):

Philadelphia	1,585,577	Reading	78,380
Pittsburgh	369,879	Bethlehem	71,428
Erie	108,718	Lancaster	55,551
Allentown	105,090	Harrisburg	52,376
Scranton	81,805	Altoona	51,881

Pennsylvania History

8,000 B.C.—People are living in Pennsylvania

A.D. 1500s—The Lenape, or Delaware, are living in southeastern Pennsylvania

1609—Henry Hudson explores Delaware Bay

1615—Cornelius Hendricksen, a Dutch explorer, sails up the Delaware River to present-day Philadelphia

1638—New Sweden is begun along the Delaware River

1655—New Sweden is captured by the Dutch; Pennsylvania becomes part of New Netherland

1664—England captures New Netherland and claims the Pennsylvania region

1681—King Charles II grants Pennsylvania to William Penn; Penn's first colonists arrive

1719—Pennsylvania's first newspaper, the *American Weekly Mercury,* is begun in Philadelphia

1731—Benjamin Franklin founds the country's first successful lending library in Philadelphia

1758—Fort Pitt, in present-day Pittsburgh, is established

1775—The Americans begin fighting the Revolutionary War against England

1776—The Declaration of Independence is adopted in Philadelphia on July 4

1783—The peace treaty that ends the Revolutionary War is signed; the United States is an independent country

1787—The U.S. Constitution is written in Philadelphia; Pennsylvania becomes the second state on December 12

1812—Harrisburg becomes Pennsylvania's permanent capital

1857—Pennsylvanian James Buchanan becomes the fifteenth president of the United States

1859—Oil is discovered near Titusville, marking the start of the world's oil industry

William Penn laying out the streets of Philadelphia

1861—The Civil War begins

1863—The Battle of Gettysburg is fought; President Lincoln makes the Gettysburg Address

1865—The North wins the Civil War

1873—Andrew Carnegie opens the country's first big steel plant near Pittsburgh

1889—The Johnstown Flood kills more than 2,200 people

1917-18—After the United States enters World War I, more than 370,000 Pennsylvanians serve; about 6,000 are killed

1941-45—After the United States enters World War II, about 1.3 million Pennsylvania men and women serve; about 27,000 die helping to win the war

1956—The Pennsylvania Turnpike, the first superhighway in the United States, is completed

1957—The country's first major nuclear power plant opens in Shippingport

1968—Pennsylvania adopts a new constitution that is still used today

1979—The country's worst nuclear accident happens at the Three Mile Island nuclear power plant near Harrisburg

1983—W. Wilson Goode is elected Philadelphia's first black mayor

1987—Pennsylvania celebrates 200 years of statehood

1988—About 1 million gallons of oil spill into the Monongahela and Ohio rivers near Pittsburgh

1990—Pennsylvania's population reaches 11,881,643

A bust of President Abraham Lincoln at Gettysburg National Cemetery

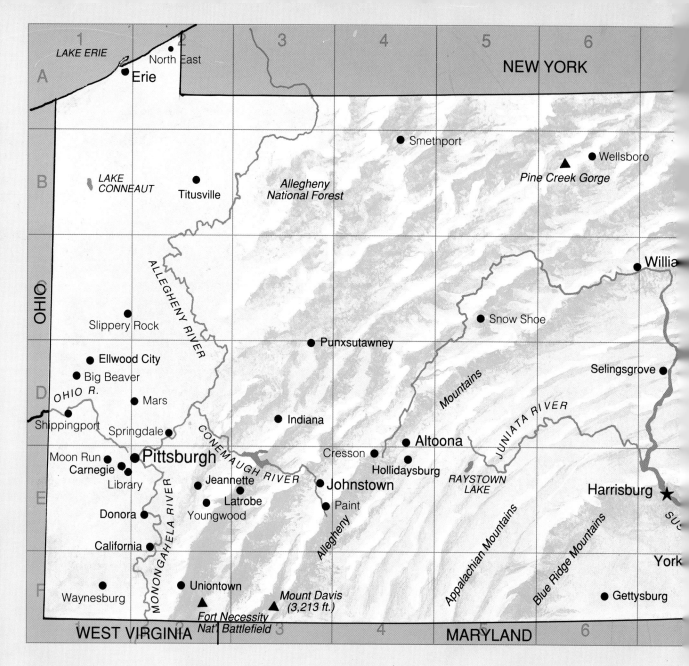

LAKE ERIE
1 2 3 4 5 6

A North East
Erie NEW YORK

B LAKE CONNEAUT Smethport Pine Creek Gorge ▲ Wellsboro
Titusville Allegheny National Forest

OHIO ALLEGHENY RIVER Willia

C Slippery Rock Snow Shoe

D Ellwood City Punxsutawney Selingsgrove
Big Beaver Mars Mountains JUNIATA RIVER
OHIO R. Springdale Indiana
Shippingport CONEMAUGH RIVER Altoona
Moon Run PITTSBURGH Cresson Hollidaysburg RAYSTOWN LAKE Harrisburg ★
Carnegie Jeannette Johnstown SUS
Library Latrobe Paint
Donora Youngwood Allegheny Appalachian Mountains York
California MONONGAHELA RIVER Blue Ridge Mountains

F Waynesburg Uniontown ▲ Mount Davis (3,213 ft.) Gettysburg
Fort Necessity Nat'l Battlefield
WEST VIRGINIA MARYLAND

OHIO D E

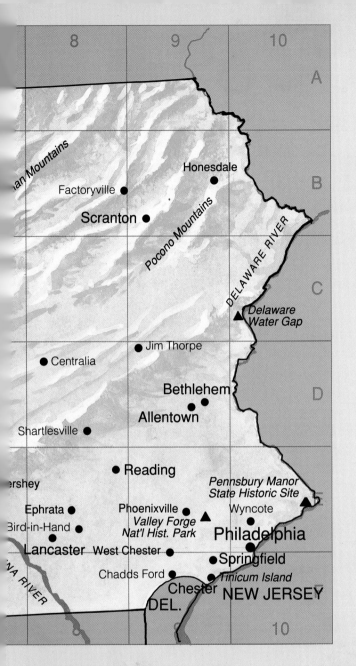

GLOSSARY

antislavery: Against slavery

billion: A thousand million (1,000,000,000)

canyon: A deep, steep-sided valley

capital: The city that is the seat of government

capitol: The building in which the government meets

climate: The typical weather of a region

colony: A settlement outside a parent country but ruled by the parent country

constitution: A framework of government

environment: The climate, soil, air, and other living things that surround us

explorer: A person who visits and studies unknown lands

fraktur: A kind of fancy lettering with designs that German people brought to Pennsylvania

glacier: A mass of slowly moving ice

Hispanic: A person of Spanish-speaking background

illustrate: To draw pictures

61

independence: Freedom

keystone: A stone in the middle of an arch that holds the other stones in place; also, something very important

labor union: A group that works for the rights of workers

locomotive: A machine that pulls railroad cars

manufacturing: The making of products

million: A thousand thousand (1,000,000)

mint: A place in which coins are made

permanent: Lasting

population: The number of people in a place

skyscraper: A very tall building

strike: Workers refusing to do their jobs in order to improve working conditions and to receive more pay

transportation: Moving goods and people by using cars, trucks, trains, ships, or airplanes

PICTURE ACKNOWLEDGMENTS

Front cover, © David Forbert; 1, © Lynn M. Stone; 2, Tom Dunnington; 3, © Joseph Nettis/Root Resources; 4-5, Tom Dunnington; 6-7, © Tom Till; 8 (left), © Tom Till; 8 (right), © Ian J. Adams/Dembinsky Photo Assoc.; 9, Courtesy of Hammond, Incorporated, Maplewood, New Jersey; 10 (left), © Ian J. Adams/Dembinsky Photo Assoc.; 10 (right), © Tom Till; 11, © Brent Parrett/N E Stock Photo; 12, © Mary Ann Brockman; 13, Historical Society of Pennsylvania; 16, © David Forbert; 17 (top), © Photri; 17 (bottom), North Wind Picture Archives, hand-colored; 18, Stock Montage, Inc.; 20, © Cameramann International, Ltd.; 21, © Joseph Nettis/Root Resources; 22, North Wind Picture Archives; 23, North Wind Picture Archives; 24, AP/Wide World Photos; 25, © K. Harriger/H. Armstrong Roberts; 26, AP/Wide World Photos; 27, © J. Nettis/H. Armstrong Roberts; 28, © Barbara L. Moore/N E Stock Photo; 29 (both pictures), Joseph Nettis/Root Resources; 30 (left), © Cameramann International, Ltd.; 30 (right), © Clyde H. Smith/N E Stock Photo; 31, © Cameramann International, Ltd.; 32-33, © David Forbert; 34, © Sam Nocella/ SuperStock; 35 (top), © Joseph Nettis/Root Resources; 35 (bottom), © Steve Elmore/Tom Stack & Associates; 36, © Tom Till; 37, © David Forbert; 38, J. Nettis/H. Armstrong Roberts; 39 (top), © Joseph Nettis/Root Resources; 39 (bottom), © Mae Scanlon; 40, © Jim Schwabel/N E Stock Photos; 41, © Joan Dunlop; 42, © Mary Ann Brockman; 43, © Tom Till; 44, North Wind Picture Archives, hand-colored; 45, Stock Montage, Inc.; 46, Stock Montage, Inc.; 47, Stock Montage, Inc.; 48, Stock Montage, Inc.; 49, Stock Montage, Inc.; 50, Wide World Photos, Inc.; 51 (top), Wide World Photos, Inc.; 51 (bottom), AP/Wide World Photos; 52, Wide World Photos, Inc.; 53, Stock Montage, Inc.; 54 (bottom), Courtesy the International Ice Cream Association; 54 (top), Philadelphia Zoo; 55, National Baseball Library and Archives, Cooperstown, N.Y.; 56 (top), Courtesy Flag Research Center, Winchester, Massachusetts 01890; 56 (middle), © Christy Volpe/mga/Photri; 56 (bottom), © Carl R. Sams, II/Dembinsky Photo Assoc.; 57 (top), © Kitty Kohout/Root Resources; 57 (bottom), © George E. Stewart/Dembinsky Photo Assoc.; 58, Stock Montage, Inc.; 59, © Cameramann International, Ltd.; 60-61, Tom Dunnington; back cover, © Gene Ahrens

INDEX

Page numbers in boldface type indicate illustrations.

ABOUT THE AUTHOR

Dennis Brindell Fradin is the author of 150 published children's books. His works for Childrens Press include the Young People's Stories of Our States series, the Disaster! series, and the Thirteen Colonies series. Dennis is married to Judith Bloom Fradin, who taught high-school and college English for many years. She is now Dennis's chief researcher. The Fradins are the parents of two sons, Anthony and Michael, and a daughter, Diana. Dennis graduated from Northwestern University in 1967 with a B.A. in creative writing, and has lived in Evanston, Illinois, since that year.